This book is intended to inspire you to write about your memories by providing you with guided suggestions.

Some questions may be difficult to answer or perhaps irrelevant, but that's okay; you may change the questions to suit your circumstances or write about why you found them tough.

You may also sketch, doodle, or use photos to bring back memories by sticking them into the pages.

In any case, have fun filling this book and giving it to your loved ones so they can keep your memories too.

Contents

Introduction

Because a mother is one-of-a-kind and irreplaceable, this book was created as a means of transfer, with the goal of strengthening the special link that exists between her and her kid.

"Verba volant, Scripta manent"
"Spoken words fly away, Written words remain."

This adage originally advised prudence, as writings, even incriminating ones, might be maintained permanently.

That proverb tells us today, in a world when everything passes us by and is rapidly forgotten, how critical it is to best retain the memory of those we love and the subtleties that make our connection so unique.

This is the goal of this book, which must be a personal account of the affectation that binds parents and their children while also assisting in the better sharing and transmission of your experiences.

DO YOU BELIEVE YOU KNOW WHO YOUR MOTHER IS?

You'd probably say yes, but consider this, she invested many years in your upbringing that you won't remember anything about. You'd be astonished to learn how much time and effort she was putting into it. Countless sleepless nights and moments have occurred. You'll only know what it's like when you're a parent.

Although you will never be able to repay your mother for everything she has done for you, the very least you can do is respect her.

It's past time for you to learn about her tale and recognize her unwavering love, unwavering dedication, and selflessness.

ARE YOU READY TO START WRITING YOUR LIFE STORY?

There are several factors that push us to sit down and try to put our tale on paper at some time. We may be attempting to make sense of it ourselves, or we may be concerned that our family history and traditions may be lost, or we may have the knowledge we want our successors to know. Whatever your motivation, now is the best moment to start. We live in a day and age where it is entirely common to work on a personal project. Perhaps you were taught as a child that talking about oneself was inappropriate, but those days are gone, and now is the time to share. In fact, if you don't, your younger family members will think you're strange! They could speak about changing their Facebook page, and now you can mention that you need to update your keepsake book page.

Writing about yourself may make you feel embarrassed or timid at first, but keep in mind that this is personal information that will only be viewed by those you choose to share it with. You may begin by working on it just while you are alone, eliminating the possibility of someone in the room asking what you are writing.

Or maybe you're not concerned at all and are eager to tell the world what you're up to. Sit down in front of your family and friends and start scribbling on these pages. Don't be startled if someone looks over your shoulder to see what you're going to put down.

What is the best place to begin? How about starting at the beginning, with your earliest childhood memories? When do you start having adult experiences in the middle? Should you begin where you are now and work your way backward? There are several entry points into life, as well as numerous stories to tell.

The questions on the next pages are designed to test your memory and help you recall decals. You'll be filling pages after pages with your memories in no time. Because writers generally run dry at some point as they rearrange the stuff on their desks for the hundredth time and dust off their laptop displays, this book is full of questions to help you get started. Alternatively, they hope the phone would ring so they could get up and answer it.

They'll get back to work as soon as the creative juices start flowing... Prompts assist authors in getting through these stumbling blocks. They provide authors with a task right away.

Close your eyes and travel back in time to attempt to remember as much detail as possible.

This is your opportunity to play the role of a reporter in your own life. Stop and consider who, what, when, where, and why with each inquiry.

So, let's go on to the following stage and begin writing about your life.

This book holds the life stories of:

....

....

Made with love by

....

Childhood

Your Arrival

Put your baby
photo in this space

Where were you born, and when?

....

....

....

....

What's the story behind your name?

....

....

....

....

What were your first words?

....

....

....

....

How did your parents describe you as a baby?

....

....

....

....

How old were your parents when you were born?

....

....

....

....

Are there any stories you were told about your birth?

....

....

....

....

What is your favorite childhood memory?

....

....

....

....

....

....

....

....

What do you know about the house you lived in as a baby? How long did you live there?

....

....

....

....

What keepsakes do you have of your early years? (ex. photos, gifts, etc...)

....

....

....

....

....

What kind of sounds and smells do you remember when you first wake up in the morning?

....

....

....

....

Is there anything you have kept from your childhood?

_____

_____

_____

_____

_____

_____

_____

What is your earliest memory?

_____

_____

_____

_____

_____

_____

_____

*What childhood fears do you remember having? For ex;
did you think were monsters under the bed, or were you
affraid of stepping on cracks?*

_____

_____

_____

_____

_____

_____

_____

*Did you have special toys or items that were precious to
you, and what's the story of how wame to you?*

_____

_____

_____

_____

_____

_____

_____

Other than your parents, were there any other adult role models in your childhood? What ade them important to you?

....

....

....

....

....

....

....

Did you have any friends whom your parents disapproved of? What caused their disapproval?

....

....

....

....

....

....

....

....

Did you often get scolded?

....

....

....

....

What were the punishments?

....

....

....

....

In short, did you have a happy childhood?

....

....

....

....

....

....

....

....

Are you sure you answered the questions correctly, because they say:

Childhood is like being drunk everyone remembers what you did except you

How many children did your parents have?

....

....

....

What was at least one important thing you learned to do or appreciate from each of your parents?

....

....

....

....

....

....

....

Growing up, who did you spend the most time with?

....

....

....

....

Did you know your grandparents?

_____

_____

_____

_____

Where did they come from, where did they grow up?

_____

_____

_____

_____

Did they teach you things, or are there things you would have liked to learn from them?

_____

_____

_____

_____

_____

_____

_____

_____

What similar or different charachter traits or personality traits did you see in your grandparents compared to your parents?

....

....

....

....

....

How did your parents spend their free time?

....

....

Are your parents strict?

....

....

Are your parents permissive or authoritative?

....

....

....

What was the best part about your family?

_____

_____

_____

_____

Did you have regular family get-togethers when you were growing up? What format did they take and how many people would come?

_____

_____

_____

_____

_____

Who was more overprotective, your mom or your dad?

_____

_____

_____

How well do you get along with your in-laws?

Who is the oldest person in your family?

Who is the funniest person in your family?

Do you usually have a family gathering?

Picture of you with your family

Happiness is having a large, loving, caring, close-knit family in another city

If the picture is bigger than the frame, please make it smaller

This family photo was taken on

__/ __/ ____

A happy *Family* is but an earlier heaven

-George Bernard Shaw-

Adolescence

How old were you when you started wearing makeup?

....
....
....

Who taught you how to apply it?

....
....
....

Did you adopt a particular dress style?

....
....
....

What kind of clothes were you wearing?

....
....
....
....
....
....

How did your personal dressing style translate?

Were you fashionable or did you follow your own style?

How did your parents react to your clothing choices?

....

....

....

....

....

....

Were you going to the theater, to the cinema, to concerts?

....

....

....

....

....

....

What were the most memorable family trips you've taken so far?

....

....

....

....

Which specific memories stand out from them?

Have you spent more or less time in other countries?

How did you describe your personality as a teenager?

What dreams and ambitions filled your heart as a teenager, and how did those shape the path you took in life? How do you hope these dreams inspire future generations in our family?

....
....
....
....
....
....

Describe a moment from your teenage years when family support meant the most to you. How did that experience strengthen your bond with your loved ones and leave a lasting legacy?

....
....
....
....
....
....
....
....

Paste a picture of
you when you were
a teenager

School

When did you start school?

....

....

....

Do you remember your first day?

....

....

....

Were you a model student or did you dislike school?

....

....

....

Who were your favorite teachers?

....

....

....

Describe why you favored them?

Paste a photo with
them if you have any,
otherwise, draw them
on a page and then
paste it here

Which school did you attend?

....

....

....

....

Who were your best friends in high school?

....

....

....

....

Picture of them

Do you still keep in touch with them?

_____

_____

_____

_____

How did you prepare to take the exams?

_____

_____

_____

_____

_____

_____

Have you ever cheated in an exam?

_____

_____

_____

_____

_____

Have you ever studied at university, if not why, if so, at which university?

....

....

....

....

....

If you had any experience at university tell me which path did you choose to study at university and why, if you had no experience at university tell me what you would have liked to study and why?

....

....

....

....

....

....

....

....

....

What are your fondest memories throughout your school or university journey?

....

....

....

....

....

....

....

....

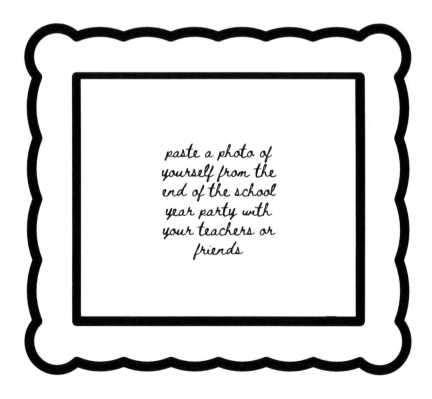

paste a photo of
yourself from the
end of the school
year party with
your teachers or
friends

How do you define love?

....

....

....

....

Do you have any personal love stories that you want to share? For ex: Your first crush or a breakup story?

....

....

....

....

....

....

Can you share the story of how you met someone who made a lasting impact on your heart? How did that relationship influence your view of love?

....

....

....

....

....

How, when and where did you meet your current partner ?

....
....

Tell me more about him, how did you meet him?

....
....
....
....
....
....
....
....
....

*Picture of
you & him*

When did you know you loved him?

....

....

....

....

What is your favorite memory with him?

....

....

....

....

....

What advice would you give to younger family members about building strong, meaningful relationships that stand the test of time? What role do love and respect play in nurturing these bonds?

....

....

....

....

....

....

When did you know you were ready for marriage?

....

....

....

What was your wedding day like?

....

....

....

What was the most meaningful lesson you learned in the early years of your marriage, and how do you hope this lesson will guide future generations in their own marriages?

....

....

....

....

....

....

....

....

....

....

Do you think people should get married in their 20's, why?

....

....

....

....

Can you describe a cherished moment from your wedding day or the beginning of your marriage? How did it set the foundation for the life and love you built together?

....

....

....

....

....

Do you believe in love at first sight?

....

....

....

....

I believe in l♡ve
at first sight

BECAUSE I

LOVE YOU

since ♡I opened

👁 *my eyes* 👁

Motherhood

How many children would you like to have?

....

....

....

What has been your greatest fear while pregnant?

....

....

....

....

....

Do you have any stories of how family & friends reacted to the news that you were going to be a mom?

....

....

....

....

....

Describe when you first knew you were going to be a mother, how did you feel?

Picture of you & me
(when I was just born)

Tell me in more detail about this photo, how old was I, what was the weather like, who took the photo for us..?

Would you like to raise your children in the way that you were raised?

....

....

....

....

In what way did your expectations of being a mom differ from your experience of being a mom?

....

....

....

....

What is the most valuable lesson motherhood has taught you that you want to pass down?

....

....

....

....

How did your upbringing influence the way you raised your children?

....

....

....

....

....

How was the first year of your motherhood?

....

....

....

....

In what ways did becoming a mom changed your life?

....

....

....

....

....

With hindsight, what advice would you give yourself today as a new mom and as a parent?

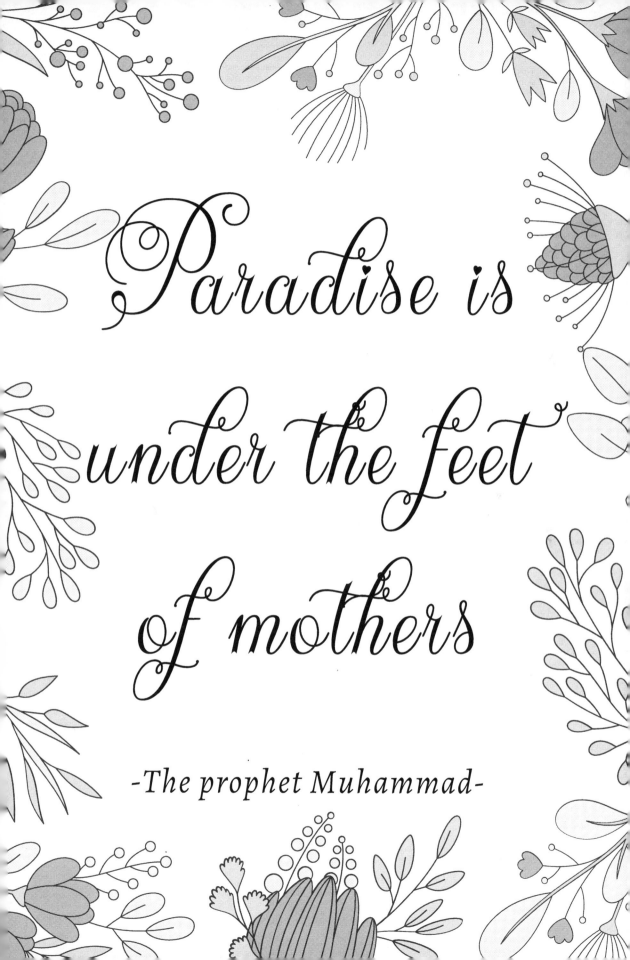

Paradise is under the feet of mothers

-The prophet Muhammad-

Activities
Entertainment

What hobbies have you had, or do you have?

....

....

....

....

....

....

When did you start and how you get into them?

....

....

....

....

....

....

Are there any dangerous hobbies?

....

....

....

....

....

_____
_____
_____
_____

Have you ever participated in contests or competitions?

_____
_____
_____
_____

Were you helping at home, what exactly were you doing? Were you enjoy doing that? If not, tell me, why you were not helping at home?

_____
_____
_____
_____
_____
_____
_____

Do you like pets? if so, what pets have you had in your life? if not, why you don't like them?

....

....

....

....

....

....

....

....

Did you ever get involved in horseplay or hijinks?

....

....

....

....

Which birthday do you remember best and why?

....

....

....

....

....

....

....

What would be your ideal way to spend the weekend?

....

....

....

....

What hobby would you get into if time and money were not an issue?

....

....

....

....

....

....

....

What kind of music did you enjoy most during your younger years, and do you have any special memories tied to those songs or artists? Can you give some examples?

....

....

....

....

....

....

....

What movies or genres did you love watching as you were growing up, and do any of them hold a special place in your heart? Can you give some examples?

....

....

....

....

....

....

....

What songs from your childhood or youth bring back the most memories?

What TV shows or characters from your past bring back fond memories, and why?

What role did the radio play in your life growing up, and do you have any special memories associated with it?

What type of movies did you enjoy watching growing up, and do you have a favorite memory of watching a movie with family or friends?

....

....

....

....

....

What romantic movies or stories have touched your heart the most, and why?

....

....

....

....

....

Are there any songs that evoke strong emotions or remind you of a significant time in your life?

....

....

....

....

Is there a Christmas that particularly marked you?

What does Mother's Day mean to you, and how has it changed over the years?

The quality

of a life is

determined by

Its Activities

Careers Jobs

How was your first job?

Did you like it or no, why ?

How old were you when you got your first job?

How much money did you earn from your first job?

....

....

Can you describe your current job or the last one?

....

....

....

....

....

....

Do you like team work, why?

....

....

....

....

Do you like working alone or in group?

....

....

....

....

....

What shift do you like to work?

....

....

....

....

Do you like working overtime?

....

....

....

....

Do you like working outdoors?

....

....

....

Have you ever been fired from a job? When? Why?

....

....

....

....

....

....

Do you work under pressure, if so, how?

....

....

....

....

Have you ever thought about starting your own business or a new business model, how did you get this idea, why?

....

....

....

....

_____

_____

_____

What's your dream job?

_____

_____

_____

_____

What plans have you made for your retirement?

_____

_____

_____

_____

How much money do you think you need to retire? Why exactly did you choose this figure, you choose it because is it sufficient for your daily needs, or for some other reasons?

_____

_____

....

....

....

....

What do you expect to enjoy doing in your retirement?

....

....

....

....

....

....

....

....

....

....

....

....

....

....

....

Thoughts Feelings

How do you define friendship?

....

....

....

....

What advice would you give for building strong and open communication within a family?

....

....

....

Who helps you pull through when life gets tough?

....

....

....

....

....

....

....

Who in your life has inspired you the most, and why?

What gets you excited about life?

What life lessons have been the most meaningful to you?

What is the difference between <u>LIVING</u> & <u>EXISTING?</u>

How old would you be if you didn't know how old you are? tell me why, and justify your answer?

....
....
....
....
....
....

If you could leave a lasting message for future generations of our family, what would it be?

....
....
....
....

What values or principles did you prioritize when raising your children, and how did you instill them in your family?

....
....
....

Do you think that money is one of the most important requirements for having a happy family?

What is your greatest quality?

What are your favorite quotes?

Write your favorite quotes

-
-
-
-

What's your main philosophy in life?

Are you currently where you want to be in life?

What are you thankful for?

I'm thankful for:

What makes you happy?

....

....

....

....

....

What makes you sad?

....

....

....

....

....

What inspires you to stay calm and collected during challenging times?

....

....

....

....

....

What advice would you give to me?

1 _____

2 _____

3 _____

What challenges in your life have taught you the greatest lessons, and how have they shaped who you are today?

Goals Wishes

What are your short-term goals?

What are your long-term goals?

Why should one set both short-term and long-term goals in order to be successful in life?

What's your biggest goal in life?

....
....
....
....
....

Why do we need goals and how can they facilitate our lives?

....
....
....
....
....

What are some different types of goals that you have achieved?

....
....
....
....
....
....

When do you give up on a goal?

Are you working on any personal development goals?

What are your top financial goals for the next 5 years?

Have you ever set spiritual goals?

....

....

....

....

....

Did you have big plans for the world or more local concerns?

....

....

....

....

....

....

....

....

....

....

....

What is a wish you have for our family's future, something you hope we'll always cherish or strive for? How can this wish be a guiding star for generations to come?

....

....

....

....

....

If you could leave behind one wish for the next generation of our family, what would it be, and why do you feel it's important for them to carry forward?

....

....

....

....

....

....

....

....

....

TO THE WORLD

you are a mom

TO OUR FAMILY

you are the world

Other Funny and Relevant Questions

What's the best prank you've ever played on someone?

....

....

....

....

....

What's the craziest dare you ever took?

....

....

....

....

....

What's your silliest memory with your best friend?

....

....

....

....

....

What's the story of your first crush?

_____

_____

_____

_____

_____

_____

If you wrote a book, what would it be called, and why?

_____

_____

_____

_____

What have you accomplished today that you are proud of?

_____

_____

_____

_____

Would you rather be able to fly in the air or breathe underwater?

....

....

....

Would you rather go a month without showering or a month without using the internet?

....

....

....

Would you rather be able to read people's minds or be able to understand anything animals say?

....

....

....

Would you prefer to live a one thousand-year-long life or ten-year-long life?

....

....

....

Would you rather be the star of a losing sports team or a benchwarmer on a winning one?

....

....

Would you choose to abolish hunger or hatred if you had the power to do it on a global scale?

....

....

Would you jump out of a plane if given the chance?

....

....

Which gemstone would you be if you were a gemstone, and why?

....

....

Which three colors are the most representative of your personality?

....

....

....

What season would you wish to remain forever, according to Justin Hayward's 1976 song "Forever Autumn"?

....

....

....

....

Do you have a fortunate number in your life?

....

....

....

....

What kind of weather do you prefer?

....

....

....

....

....

What's the worst present you've ever gotten?

....

....

....

What's the most amusing thing you've ever overheard?

....

....

....

Which of your phone's apps is the most helpful, and which is the least useful yet entertaining?

....

....

....

....

What's the most ridiculous thing your parents ever did to embarrass you?

....

....

....

What were words you couldn't pronounce as a child, so you made up your own?

....

....

....

What was the most recent event that completely blew your mind?

....

....

....

What do you pretend to hate but actually love?

....

....

What's the craziest thing on your bucket list?

....

....

....

Everyone has those nightmares that come back to haunt them. What is your worst fear? what is your nightmare?

_____

_____

_____

_____

_____

_____

How long has it been since you owed someone money?

_____

_____

_____

Have you ever lied to impress someone with a talent or an interest? What occurred after that?

_____

_____

_____

_____

If you could snap your fingers and become an expert in something, what would you want it to be? Why?

....
....
....
....
....

What simple pleasures of life do you truly enjoy?

....
....
....
....

What is one of your worst habits?

....
....
....
....

Do you have a lucky number? If so, what is it? Why?

....
....

What makes a birthday special for you?

....
....
....
....

Letters to Family and Friends

You may use this place to write letters to your loved ones.

My love,

For all the times I haven't thanked you, whether because I was too young, too busy, or just couldn't find the words, now I want to express my gratitude, and to thank you for all you've done for me. Now that I'm older I realize more and more everything you did, everything you gave, and most importantly, everything you stand for, and I love you and thank you with all of my heart.

Your little love

We create our books with love & great care.
Yet mistakes can always happen.
For any issues with your journal, such as faulty binding, printing errors,
suggestions, or any questions regarding our books, please do not hesitate to
contact us at: *tankrabooks@gmail.com*

Without your voice, we don't exist.
Please, support us and leave a review!

Thank you!